BUGS

by Oscar Gake

Harcourt

Orlando   Boston   Dallas   Chicago   San Diego

Visit *The Learning Site!*

www.harcourtschool.com

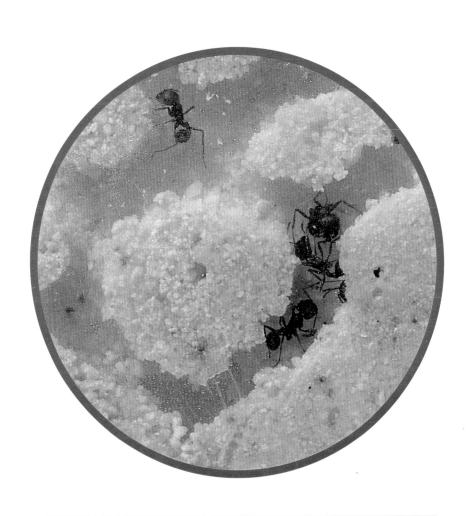

Some bugs dig.

Some bugs sting.

Some bugs hop.

Some bugs fly.

Some bugs make webs.

Some bugs walk.

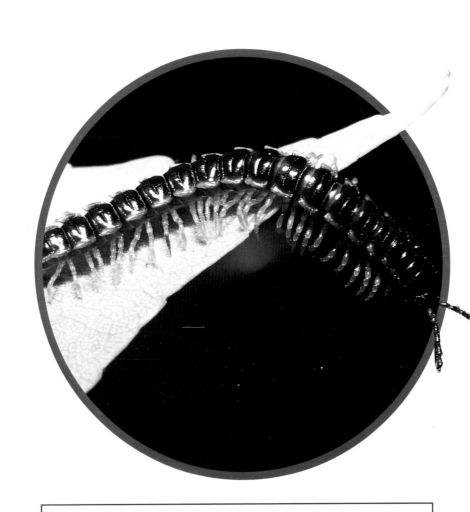

Some bugs walk
very fast!